I am a Golden Buddha

A Journey from Self-Criticism to Inner Peace

JENNY MESSERLE

I am a Golden Buddha: a Journey from Self-Criticism to Inner Peace
by Jenny Messerle

© 2016 Jenny Messerle

For more information about this book or the author, visit www.jennymesserle.com

ISBN 978-1530069262
1. Self-Acceptance 2. Self-Esteem 3. Happiness I. Title

First edition
Printed in the United States of America

To Ian.
I am the person I am today
because of your unconditional love.

Contents

Introduction   1

Section one: The story of the golden Buddha   5

Section two: I discover something wrong with my thoughts about myself   11

Section three: I identify the ways that I think something is wrong with me; instead of criticizing myself, I appreciate myself   17

Gratitude   143

About the author   144

Request   145

Notes   147

Introduction

In my thirties, I found another source of happiness.

Before this discovery, I believed two things about happiness:

1. Happiness is a positive feeling, such as joy, bliss, fulfillment, or gratitude.
2. Diligence is the path to happiness.

Because of these beliefs, I worked at the following:

- I identified what things made me smile and laugh and I scheduled them into my life.
- I set and achieved goals.
- I carved out and committed to time with family and friends.
- I reminded myself to find the good in a challenging moment, person, or day.

I believed in the power of effort so much that even when another person's behavior or my circumstances clashed with my hopes, I believed that if I obsessed about it enough, I could change things. Even though trying to control what was outside of my control was futile, this mental focus was still effort. And, any effort kept me on the path to getting what I wanted.

* * * * *

When I discovered the Serenity Prayer, I longed to understand how to apply its insight to my life:

> God grant me the serenity
> To accept the things I cannot change;
> Courage to change the things I can;
> And the wisdom to know the difference.

If I could not change my circumstances, I would learn how to change my attitude.

*   *   *   *   *

When I was thirty-two years old, I began practicing yoga. Through yoga, I learned to notice my feelings and my thoughts in the present moment. I realized that neither other people nor my circumstances create the feelings of frustration, anxiousness, and inadequacy that I feel. I am the one who adds these unhappy feelings to my life.

This was when I discovered another source of happiness: contentment or inner peace. Contentment is to feel less unhappiness every day. Contentment is to feel less frustration, less stress, and less inadequacy in my life.[1]

With this discovery, I decided to identify how to experience more contentment and less self-added unhappiness in my life.

*   *   *   *   *

On my journey, I discovered how attachment can create unhappiness and how non-attachment can create contentment.

- Attachment is being fixated on attaining a certain result. Attachment is also obsessing about avoiding something I don't want. When the actual or likely result differs from my wishes, I feel frustrated, anxious, or regretful.

- Non-attachment is being okay with whatever happens. Non-attachment is letting go of wanting what I originally wanted and choosing inner peace instead.

As I practiced non-attachment in my life, I felt more contentment. I learned to find inner peace:

- On rainy days when I craved sunshine;
- In traffic jams and long lines when I wanted efficiency;
- In crowded movie theatres and yoga classes when my body longed to be in my favorite spot in the room;
- When I created bland drawings and mediocre paintings and I yearned to make beautiful art;
- When we moved back to Seattle and my husband couldn't find a job; and
- When I hurt my left heel and stopped running for two years and I didn't know when I would run again.

In these short, ordinary moments and longer periods of time, I uncovered contentment underneath the frustration, impatience, and hopelessness.

*   *   *   *   *

Even though I was happier than I was earlier in my life, I knew that my days still held a lot of self-added unhappiness. As I continued to pay attention to my feelings, I identified one large part of my life when I often felt out-of-sorts: interactions with other people.

I knew that when I talked with, emailed, or was merely in the presence of another person, there were things that I wanted and things that I didn't want in the experience. If I could identify and let go of these things, then I could enjoy my time with other people.

*   *   *   *   *

This book explains how I turn feelings of self-consciousness and inadequacy into inner peace and how I reshape self-criticism into self-appreciation. The secrets of these transformations are to:

- Identify the things I don't want in social interactions, such as what I'm afraid other people will think of me;
- Dispel these fears;
- Adopt affirmations of my value; and
- See myself as a whole and worthy person or see myself as a golden Buddha.

This book explains these secrets in more detail.

Section one:

The story of the golden Buddha

The story of the golden Buddha

In the fourteenth century, sculptors created a golden Buddha statue for a Thai monastery. The statue was ten feet tall and ten feet wide from knee to knee. For three hundred years, the golden Buddha glowed and radiated.

In 1757, when the Thai monks learned of an impending invasion by the Burmese army, the monks covered the Buddha statue with a thick layer of clay. In some parts of the clay surface, the clay was eight inches thick.

During the attack, the monks were killed and the monastery was ransacked. But the Buddha statue was left untouched. For two hundred years, the Buddha statue existed as a clay Buddha and the secret of its golden nature remained hidden.

In 1955, the Thai monks decided to move the Buddha across the monastery grounds. To lift the statue, the monks tied ropes around the idol and developed a pulley system. Dozens of men pulled on the ropes to raise the statue. During the move, one of the ropes broke and the Buddha fell to the earth and a crack formed in the surface.

When the monks examined the crack, they saw a glimmer of gold. In the glimpse of the statue's surface, the monks realized that their statue was not a clay Buddha but a metal Buddha covered with clay.

To restore the statue to its original state, the monks used hammers and chisels and chipped away at the clay. As more and more of the clay was removed, the Buddha statue shined brighter and brighter.

After the monks finished their work, the full brilliance of the Buddha statue was revealed. The Buddha was a ten-foot high, ten-foot wide statue of pure gold![2]

A glimpse of my Buddha nature

Not that long ago, I discovered that I believed something was inherently wrong with me. This belief explained why I felt self-conscious and inadequate around other people.

A month after this discovery, I learned about the golden Buddha.

Together, these two experiences made me realize the following:

- In my upbringing, I internalized certain beliefs about myself. These beliefs are undesirable attributes that I'm afraid other people will think of me.
- The accumulation of these attributes made me believe that something is wrong with me and made me worry that other people will see something wrong with me too. That is the reason why I don't feel confident or comfortable around other people. These beliefs are like the clay layers that hide the Buddha statue's worth.
- If I want to feel at ease around other people, I need to unearth the undesirable attributes from my subconscious, see them as untruths, and reject them from my self-identity. Then, I can see myself as the whole and worthy person I am. Like the golden Buddha, I will restore my self-image to its original brilliance.

In the next section of this book, I describe the key insights related to how I discovered something wrong with my thoughts about myself.

In the last section of this book, section three, I identify the ways that I think something is wrong with me. As I rejected these beliefs, I learned to appreciate myself instead of criticize myself and I began to see myself as a golden Buddha. In section three, I also explain how my self-critical beliefs formed during my upbringing and how the beliefs reproduced and camouflaged themselves throughout my life.

Section two:

I discover something wrong with my thoughts about myself

Childhood messages

During a class taught by the artist Erin Faith Allen,[3] I had an "aha" moment. Erin encouraged us to remember the messages that people told us when we were growing up and she asked us to complete this journaling prompt: "You are ..."

Below are the words I wrote in my journal:

- You're weird.
- You worry too much.
- You're ugly.
- You're boring.
- You're lazy.

The biggest revelation for me was the adjective *weird*. Seeing the words "You're weird" made me realize the following:

- I believe that I am weird and that it's a shameful characteristic.
- I'm afraid that I will say something or act in a way that people will think is weird. I worry that people will privately or publicly criticize me for being weird and will shun me.
- I avoid talking with people whenever I can. I prefer for people to think that I am shy, too tired, or too busy to socialize than for people to think that I am weird.

- After conversations, I replay them in my mind. I obsess about what I should or shouldn't have said.

- I carry the inner criticism and inadequate feeling with me. Then, when I have time, I run for several miles to purge the self-judgment and out-of-sort feelings. I sleep eight to ten hours to reset my mind.

Then I wake up and I repeat the same process over again: worrying that people think I'm weird, judging myself for being weird, purging my thoughts, resetting my mind, worrying, judging, purging, resetting…

I also practice these habits for other adjectives, such as *boring* and *lazy*.

I realized that it was time to change how I approached my life.

*   *   *   *   *

"There is nothing that is a more certain sign of insanity than to do the same thing over and over and expect the results to be different." Albert Einstein

Energy

I get more energy by being by myself than by being with other people.

For decades, I thought that this is because I am an introvert. As a result, I subconsciously used my introvert identity as an excuse to escape social interactions. If I avoided being with people, then I avoided the depleting effects of these experiences.

But with all of this evasion, I also avoided the root cause of why it drains me to email, talk, and be with other people. When I am around others:

- I continually worry that people will find something wrong with what I said or did and, as a result, will believe that there is something wrong with me as a person.
- I judge other people and I get annoyed at their behavior and at them (and then I judge myself for being so petty).
- I worry about saying or doing something that will hurt other people's feelings or will offend them.

With all of these self-criticisms, judgments, and worries, it makes sense why it exhausts me to interact with other people.

When I am by myself, I am mainly free of inner critics. This is the main reason why I get more energy by being by myself than by being with other people.

Special

When I attended a workshop led by the author Sabrina Ward Harrison,[4] we wrote about childhood memories. Below is what I wrote to the journaling prompt: "When I was six..."

> When I was six, I started at Mountville Elementary School. It was a new school for me. My mom sent me to school with a box of red Twizzlers. I drew rainbows and flowers and my new classmates loved me. Two boys told me that they wanted to marry me.
>
> I don't remember much else from that year or from my elementary school years.
>
> I see how the memories that stick out for me are the memories when I felt special or I didn't feel special. That is what I seek in life—to feel special and to make other people feel special. What I fear in life is that I am unworthy because that is how I feel more often than I'd like.

When I wrote the above journal entry, I discovered something that had been hidden from me until that moment: I believe that there is something inherently wrong with me.

Because I believe that there is something inherently wrong with me, it is easy for me to feel self-conscious and inadequate around other people. This belief is the source of my inner critics.

Self-fulfilling prophecies

If I believe that something is wrong with me, this belief is shame. Shame is a belief of unworthiness and inferiority.[5]

Shame is also a fear. Like many fears, shame can become a self-fulfilling prophecy.

In psychology, this process is called confirmation bias. If I have an idea about the accuracy of a certain belief, with confirmation bias:

- I will stop seeing evidence that disagrees with my belief.
- I will only see evidence that confirms my belief's accuracy.

Confirmation bias works whether my belief is in my conscious or subconscious mind.

Section three:

I identify the ways that I think something is wrong with me; instead of criticizing myself, I appreciate myself

THERE ARE EIGHT AREAS OF MY LIFE IN WHICH I FEEL VERY SELF-CONSCIOUS.

Shame-related feelings

Shame is a belief and shame is also a feeling. For me, I experience this spectrum of shame-related feelings when I email, talk with, or am around other people:

uneasiness➔ self-consciousness➔inadequacy➔anxiety➔ shame

Each feeling is a lesser form of the shame feeling. And the sources of each feeling are self-shaming thoughts—thoughts telling me that there is something wrong with me.

Gateways to the subconscious

Unhappy feelings are gateways to understanding subconscious self-critical thoughts. This is because feeling inadequate is like having a fever; both conditions indicate an underlying unaddressed issue.[6]

But for most of life, I was unaware of the value of examining my feelings. Whenever I felt inadequate or anxious, I disregarded my emotional inner world and I paid attention to whatever was going on in my physical outer world. I focused on the conversation I was having, the project I was working on at my job, or the errands I needed to finish before dinner.

If I had time to spare, I used that opportunity to escape from my discomfort. I walked ten minutes to a bakery to buy a five-inch iced pumpkin cookie and maybe a zucchini muffin. And maybe a coconut macaroon too. I'd fill the time before my walk and the twenty-minute trip to the bakery and back with the happiness of anticipation. But within a few minutes after I finished bingeing on my baked goods, my original inadequate feeling returned. But then I also felt guilty, ashamed, and bloated, and I had an awful sugar low.

* * * * *

Since thoughts create feelings, if I notice when I feel uneasy, self-conscious, inadequate, or ashamed, then I can identify the self-critical thoughts and shame beliefs that are the root causes. This is how I will discover the ways that I think something is wrong with me.

Shame labels and shame sources

As I pay attention to my unhappy feelings, I realize that each period of self-deprecation lasts a few seconds or a few minutes. But I fill up each day with dozens of these self-inflicted moments of inadequacy.

When I study these moments, I find what I'm afraid other people will think of me. For example, I may worry that someone will view me as selfish or lazy. The attributes that I worry about are my shame labels. My shame labels are usually negative adjectives—adjectives with undesirable connotations associated with them.

When I identify themes in my shame labels, I discover the sources of my shame beliefs: my shame sources.[7] In this section, I learn that my shame sources include the following:

- Actions such as pursuing new friendships, making decisions, and making requests;

- Components of my identity such as being Asian, my character, and my social and economic background; and

- Social expectations such as being courteous and helpful.

Like the clay layers over the Buddha statue, my shame labels hide my worth. If I uncover my shame labels and shame sources, I will find the causes of my self-criticism. If I reject the shame labels from my identity, I will reveal the brilliance of my inherent Buddha nature.

How this section is organized

This section contains over twenty examples of when I felt some form of unhappiness between uneasiness and shame. In each situation, I discovered the shame label that caused the feeling and I selected an affirmation to adopt. In some stories, I identified insight about how my shame belief reproduces or camouflages itself.

I've noticed eight parts of my life that tend to make me feel uneasy, self-conscious, inadequate, or ashamed. I consider these my shame sources:

1. Pursuing friendships
2. Being Asian
3. My character
4. Decisions and comprehension
5. Making requests
6. Being courteous
7. Being helpful
8. My social and economic background

In this section, I grouped my stories by shame source and I arranged the shame sources in the order in which I discovered them. My shame sources are more like overlapping layers than interlocking pieces. The initial shame sources were easier to detect and the latter ones were less apparent. I was able to unearth the latter buried shame sources because I had first uncovered the initial surface layers.

For example:

- This section's first story relates to shame source #1, *Pursuing friendships*. In that story, it was clear to me that a belief of unworthiness is the root of my self-criticism.

- While writing the essays for shame sources #6 and #7, I realized that I derive my identity and sense of worth from being courteous and helpful. When I don't feel courteous enough or helpful enough, I feel inadequate.

Shame source #1:
Pursuing
Friendships

New friends

I love making new friends.

But in these pursuits, it's also easy for me to feel unworthy and rejected, especially if the person doesn't email me back or doesn't reciprocate my enthusiasm in keeping in touch. Also, while I wait for a reply to my email, I fill the waiting time with self-doubts and I imagine the person laughing and thinking, "Who does Jenny think she is? Why would I want to be *friends* with her?"

But there are many reasons why people don't respond to emails or aren't interested in a new friendship. And these reasons may be independent from how the person feels about me and are definitely independent from my value as a person and as a potential friend.

Even if a person accepts my lunch invitation, I worry that it's because she's just being nice and polite. I worry that she's actually not looking forward to spending time with me.

Why do I fill the beginning phases of new friendships with such self-skepticism? Why do I mistrust that a person would be interested in being my friend?

*   *   *   *   *

Throughout my life, I have many memories in which I pursued a friendship and felt unwanted. As I reflect on my life, one attempted friendship stands out in my mind.

I was in college. I was a sophomore or a junior, which was 1995 or 1996. Her name was Tina. I forget how I met Tina or how we started to hang out together. I do remember that our friendship coincided with a difficult period with my boyfriend. My boyfriend attended a school that was four hours away from my college. I remember crying to Tina about my boyfriend and her reassuring me.

I also remember the morning of Tina's birthday.

I borrowed my roommate's stash of streamers and balloons and I walked to Tina's dorm.

When I approached the door of Tina's suite, the door was open. I didn't peer through the door to see if anyone was in the common room or if the bedroom doors were open or closed. Since I only had a few minutes before my class started, I began twisting the pink and purple crepe streamers together and taping them along the door frame. Then I taped the four purple balloons and a handwritten birthday sign to the top of the door.

As I gathered my supplies and prepared myself to leave, I heard Tina's suitemate say, "I saw Jenny walk by with balloons. Are you friends with her?"

Then I heard Tina say, "No. Not really."

I thought, " 'No. Not really.' What a fool you have been Jenny! Who would want to be friends with you? All those times that you hung out with Tina—it was because she felt sorry for you. It was because she pitied you and was just comforting a fellow woman in need. It wasn't because she *liked* you or wanted to be your friend. How could you be so blind to mistake her actions for anything other than pity?"

*　　*　　*　　*　　*

Whenever I worry that someone will interpret me or my actions as needy or pitiful, I remind myself that I am a big-hearted person. I'd rather go through life—pursuing friendships, lavishing people with compliments, being enamored with people I meet, and giving unconditional love—than to stop seeking these connections.

Life is not about expressing just enough love as I think I will receive.

Yes, sometimes I'll feel rejected. Yes, sometimes attempted friendships won't work out. And yes, sometimes I'll like or love someone more than she likes me.

But sometimes my efforts will yield beautiful friendships that will fill my life with more joy than I could have imagined.

*　　*　　*　　*　　*

When I find myself worrying that someone thinks I am needy or pitiful, I repeat the shame labels and I imagine them falling off of my body. "I am not a needy or pitiful person. I am not a needy or pitiful person. I am not a needy or pitiful person."

Sometimes I add a prerequisite step and I visualize myself unearthing these shame labels from my subconscious and then purging them from my identity. "I am not a needy or pitiful person. I am not a needy or pitiful person. I am not a needy or pitiful person."

After I recognize and reject my shame labels, I repeat a self-affirming mantra, such as "I am a big-hearted and loveable person. I am a big-hearted and loveable person. I am a big-hearted and loveable person." With each mantra, I imagine myself absorbing the words into my identity and seeing the words coat the space where the shame label used to cover.

I also picture each mantra as a polish that highlights the brilliance of my inherent golden Buddha self. This way, each mantra is a reminder that I am a golden Buddha.

I am a golden Buddha. I am a golden Buddha. I am a golden Buddha.

Shame source #2:
Being Asian

Toilet seat covers

Whenever another woman enters a toilet stall after me and I hear the sound of crinkling paper, I think, "She's using a toilet seat cover because I used the toilet before her." And for a minute, I feel very small. I have these thoughts and feelings even if the person is a coworker or a friend.

When I wrote about this experience, three questions arose:

1. What adjective am I worried that she thinks of me?

I'm afraid that she thinks I'm dirty and she doesn't want to catch anything from me.

2. I am thirty-eight years old. Why did it take me this long to realize that I have this belief?

A lot of thoughts are in my subconscious and all I'm aware of is the feeling. By the time I finish drying my hands, the feeling has disappeared.

3. Where did my fear come from? Why do I worry that people think I'm contaminated?

As a child, I remember taking a bath at my babysitter's house. I remember the shiny white tub and how the brown square tiles stretched from the edge of the tub to the ceiling. I remember how my feet stopped sliding when I stood on the gray plastic flower shapes stuck to the bottom of the tub. I remember my babysitter saying, "Okay, Jenny all done" and her stretching open a white towel for me. I also remember her saying to me, "Don't use the towel on your privates."

Looking back on this memory, I wonder if she would have said those same words to me if I was also white. Or, if she only said that to Asians.

As a child, I found it confusing that someone who told me that she loved me and would hug me tightly whenever she saw me wouldn't let her towels touch certain parts of my body.

How old was I?

I don't remember. But too young to safely take a bath by myself.

*   *   *   *   *

When examining this experience, a useful mantra arose: "Her action is unrelated to me." This mantra is helpful because I tend to view other people's actions as direct responses to my preceding behavior. But this interpretation is a faulty one. Just because two actions occur contemporaneously, it doesn't mean there is a cause and effect relationship between them.

"Her action is unrelated to me. Her action is unrelated to me. Her action is unrelated to me."

When I think "Her action is unrelated to me," I am disconnecting two events:

- First event: I exit a toilet stall.
- Second event: The woman uses a toilet seat cover.

But when I disconnect two events, my mind wants to connect the second event to something, anything, because that is how my mind works. My mind is hard-wired to connect events to create stories. To help the disconnecting action be effective, I need to think of an alternative story for the second event to connect to:

- Maybe she acts this way all the time regardless of who is around. This time it happened to be me. I'm an observer, not the cause of her action.
- Maybe she always uses a toilet seat cover whenever they're available.
- Maybe she has a higher than normal fear of germs in public places and she's the kind of person who opens doors with paper towels, carries hand sanitizer in her pocket, and has antibacterial hand wipes in her purse.

*   *   *   *   *

Her action is unrelated to me.

I am not dirty or contaminated.

I am pure and clean. I am pure and clean. I am pure and clean.

With each affirmation, I am reminding myself I am a golden Buddha.

I am a golden Buddha. I am a golden Buddha. I am a golden Buddha.

Credit cards

Sometimes when I pay with a credit card and the cashier asks, "May I see your ID?" I think, "Are you asking me because I'm Asian? You didn't ask the previous customer to see his ID. He was white."

I want to say these words out loud.

But I'm afraid that whatever confused look the cashier gives me or her hesitation in her response will just cement my suspicion.

*   *   *   *   *

Her action is unrelated to me.

I am not an untrustworthy person. I am not an inferior person.

I am an ethical, honorable, and worthy person. I am an ethical, honorable, and worthy person. I am an ethical, honorable, and worthy person.

With each affirmation, I am reminding myself I am a golden Buddha.

I am a golden Buddha. I am a golden Buddha. I am a golden Buddha.

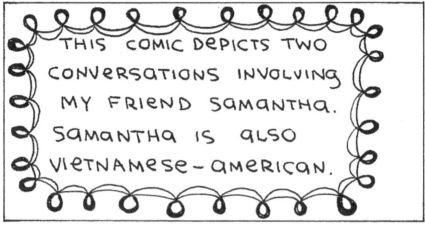

ALL MY LIFE, MY MOM & AUNTS KEPT TELLING ME: NO WHITE GUY IS GOING TO BE INTERESTED IN YOU. IF HE IS, IT'S BECAUSE YOU'RE A NOVELTY. HE'S NEVER GOING TO BE SERIOUS ABOUT YOU & INTRODUCE YOU TO HIS MOM OR MARRY YOU.

IVE BEEN OPERATING UNDER THIS BELIEF FOR SO MANY YEARS. WHENEVER I PURSUED A GUY & IF HE WASN'T INTERESTED, I THOUGHT, "IT'S BECAUSE IM ASIAN."

FIFTEEN YEARS LATER: AS I REFLECT BACK ON MY CONVERSATION WITH SAMANTHA, I WONDER, "I FEEL SHAME ABOUT BEING ASIAN. WHAT ARE OTHER WAYS THAT BEING ASIAN INFLUENCES HOW I INTERPRET OTHER PEOPLE'S ACTIONS?"

Mountville Elementary School

After I realized that I feel shame about being Asian, three memories from my elementary school years arose:

Memory #1: The lunch box

When I was in elementary school, I brought my lunch to school in a plastic blue Smurfs lunch box. I don't remember which years I used that same lunch box, but I remember the image: Smurfette, Papa Smurf, and six other Smurfs. In the scene, Smurfette stood on a yellow-orange mushroom and wore a gold crown and a pink robe trimmed with white fur. Each Smurf held a gift for her, such as a piece of cake, a mug of frothy root beer, or a pink box wrapped with red satin ribbon. Over the years, the image lost its glossy finish and the edges peeled away from the lunch box surface. Even in its faded state, the scene always made me smile.

After we ate our lunches and before we went to recess, we stacked our empty lunch boxes into a large cardboard box displaying our teacher's name. Stacks of these oversized cardboard boxes lined tables in the corner of the cafeteria.

At the end of recess, assigned students carried the boxes to the classrooms. Before the end of the day, each student collected his or her lunch box.

One day, when I grabbed my lunch box, I noticed that it was heavier than it was a few hours earlier. For a moment, I wondered if I was holding someone else's possession in my hands. But I knew it was mine. I was the only student with a faded blue plastic Smurfs lunch box. Most students had tin lunch boxes. Favorite themes included E.T., The A- Team, The Muppets, Scooby-Doo, and Knight Rider.

When I opened the lid, I noticed that someone had put something inside.

I saw the chocolate-colored pile of mush that looked like brown lumpy mashed potatoes. From the stench, I recognized what it was.

Memory #2: The playground:

In second grade, most students loved recess break. But I didn't.

Recess time meant opportunities to play kickball, tetherball, or four square. Recess was also a chance to sit and talk with your best friend. But when you didn't have a best friend or weren't athletic, recess was a reminder that you didn't fit in.

Whenever the recess bell rang, all of my movements slowed down. I took twice as long as usual to put away my books, to walk from my desk to my locker, and to put on my jacket and zip it up. If I was the last student on the playground, then I could see where everyone else had settled for the recess break. This was the best way for me to survey the area to find an isolated spot to sit and to be by myself. Sometimes I leaned against a tree. Sometimes I sat against the brick wall of the school building. Sometimes I rested on my back on the grass and stared at the moving cloud shapes.

One day, as I walked toward my chosen site, I spotted a boy sitting against the wall. He wore a plain gray crew neck sweatshirt and blue jeans. He just sat there with his legs stretched out in front of him and his back against the bricks. As I walked by him, I looked over and smiled at him.

But instead of smiling back, he waved his arms and shouted at me: "Chinese! Japanese! Look at these! Chinese! Japanese! Look at these!" As he barked this rhyme, his arms and fingers alternated between two movements:

- In his first movement, he extended his pointer fingers and pressed them on his forehead a centimeter from the outside corners of his eyes and he pulled the skin diagonally upward to create slants with his eyes.

- In his second movement, he pinched his thumbs and pointer fingers together to squeeze his sweatshirt fabric. He grabbed at the area where his nipples were and he pulled the gray cloth outward to create imaginary breasts.

As he chanted, "Chinese! Japanese!" he created slants with his eyes, tilted his head to the right, and made a grimace-like grin. When he yelled, "Look at these!" he created the illusion of breasts.

It wasn't until I was out of his sight that I stopped hearing his voice.

Memory #3: The shade

During the summer before third grade, I attended YMCA camp at my elementary school. On Friday afternoons, the ice cream truck visited and kids spent their allowances on ice cream sandwiches, orange creamsicles, or chocolate fudge bars. My favorite was the strawberry shortcake ice cream bar from Good Humor. I ate the bar in layers. First, I ate the outside pink and white cookie-crumb coating until the ragged white middle layer remained. Then, bite after bite, I finished off the vanilla layer with its strawberry interior.

I usually ate my ice cream under a specific tree, a twenty-foot tall oak tree along the perimeter of the school grounds. In this spot, I was shaded from the sun and I could be alone. Since the tree overlooked the playground, I would be able to see my camp counselor waving at me to rejoin the group. From this location, I could also observe the cars that passed by the school.

As I neared the last bite of strawberry ice cream that clung to the wooden popsicle stick, I heard shouting.

I looked up and saw a brown station wagon with thin yellow and white horizontal stripes. As the car approached me, I saw two boys leaning out of the rear passenger seat window. The hems of their white T-shirts flapped in the wind as their hands held onto the roof of the car. It wasn't until the car had passed me that I registered the words they had been repeating over and over again: "Ching Chong! Ching Chong! Ching Chong!"

<u>Realization about my shame source of being Asian:</u>

Somewhere in my life, I suppressed these three memories and I forgot about them. I'm not sure exactly when this happened. But I have a guess. I also have a hunch of how it happened.

I grew up in the suburbs of Lancaster, Pennsylvania. The community was predominantly white. For example, in my graduating class of over four hundred students, there were only fourteen Asians and few other people of color. During my middle school and high school years, if I walked alone on a sidewalk or across a field, I felt uneasy when I saw a group of boys and no one else around. I never feared for my safety. But in those situations, I worried that the boys would shout some racial slur at me.

When I was twenty-one, I moved four hours west to Pittsburgh. Pittsburgh also had a large white population and a tiny Asian one. I worked downtown at an accounting firm. During my lunch breaks, I walked alone to window-shop or to visit art galleries. Sometimes I'd walk by a lone man and as I passed by him, he'd spit the word "Chink!" at me.

When I was twenty-six, my husband, Ian, and I moved across the country to Seattle. After my first day of work, I told Ian, "Out of the sixteen people in my department, there are six other Asians! Six! Can you believe it?" During my thirteen years in Seattle, no one has ever said anything racially offensive to me.

The absence of racist slurs and actions is why I forgot that I feel shame about being Asian.

Realization about my shame sources:

In general, shame labels and shame sources are elusive. One reason they are difficult to identify is because I've suppressed the associated shameful memories. Since I'm a visual person, it's easier for me to remember memories with a visual component. If a memory has an associated image, the image becomes a handle for me to pull the memory out of my subconscious into my conscious mind.

Regarding shameful memories about being Asian: For each of the three elementary school stories, I can visualize the experience. For example, I can picture fingers pulling eyes into slants and I can imagine the brown lumpy mush inside my lunch box.

When I wrote the essay *New friends*, the image of me decorating Tina's door with streamers surfaced without effort. I tried and tried to summon more examples of when someone else made me feel unwanted. But I couldn't. I wasn't able to remember any other specific situation. I couldn't recall the names of the kids who shunned me or the physical settings of when I felt cast off.

This is because each moment of rejection looks like one of any thousands of experiences that I've had in my life. If you take a photograph of an event when I was shunned and compare it to a situation when I was just hanging out with other kids, in each photograph you would see silhouettes of kids. There would be no apparent distinguishing characteristics between the two photos. But if you look carefully at the photo depicting when I was rebuffed, you would see a hurt look in my eyes and a downturned head. If you examined the other child's face, you would see her annoyance as she rolled her eyes and you would notice that her head was rotating away from me. But other than these subtle facial and body hints, there would be no noteworthy visual features in the shameful situations to help me collect them from my memory.

Observable visual signs would also be missing from the hundreds of times when an adult or peer criticized me or made me feel that I had done or said something inappropriate or that something was wrong with me.

Despite how easy it is for me to feel self-conscious, inadequate, or ashamed, it is challenging for me to remember the specific past situations that created my beliefs of inferiority and unworthiness. If I cannot recall these memories, then I cannot examine them for clues about my shame labels and shame sources.

*   *   *   *   *

People will forget what you said.
People will forget what you did.
But people will never forget how you made them feel.

\-   Maya Angelou

Shame source #3:
My character

The internet and the recycle bin

Sometimes when I'm at work, I imagine a person standing behind me checking up on me to make sure that I'm working. In these moments of paranoia, I think, "See, I'm working. I'm diligent. I'm not slacking off or surfing the internet. I'm good. I'm not bad."

*   *   *   *   *

One morning, before my co-workers and manager arrived, I cleared out my navy blue L.L.Bean book bag. I found a three-inch by five-inch Post-it Note that said "internet to do items" at the top and all of the items were crossed off. As I threw the Post-it Note into the cardboard recycle bin under my desk, I felt uneasy and I noticed this thought: "What if, after I leave work today, my manager rummages through my recycle bin to look for evidence of me spending work time doing personal things?" Since my manager would never perform this action, I wanted to understand the source of my paranoia.

*   *   *   *   *

During high school, my mom eavesdropped on my phone calls (with my friends, boyfriend, and even with my dad), read my diary, called friends' parents to confirm that I was at their house, and rummaged through my trash and laundry hamper. My mom made me feel like I was an inherently disobedient and dubious person and that she was going to catch me doing something wrong to prove her suspicions about me.

In addition to my mom, my peers also fed my paranoid belief that people are inherently suspicious of other people's character:

- As a teenager, many conversations focused on badmouthing someone who wasn't in the room.
- In my first job after college graduation, my coworkers often criticized the behavior and character flaws of the people we worked with.

* * * * *

My social paranoia was similar to a murder mystery in which all of the townspeople suspect a specific person to be the killer. Since the townspeople cannot prove this person's questionable worth, they scrutinize her behavior in hopes of catching her doing just one thing wrong to evidence that she is indeed a bad person.

But my life is not a murder mystery. No one privately or publicly suspects my character. No one obsessively scrutinizes my behavior. No one walks around all day thinking, "There is something wrong with Jenny and I'm going to prove it."

* * * * *

When I compared my social paranoia to a murder mystery, I finally understood how perfectionism works:

- In my life, I aim for perfect behavior. This is because perfect behavior proves to me that there is *nothing* wrong with me.
- If my behavior is less than perfect, I believe that this confirms that there is *something* wrong with me. For example, if a coworker walks by my cubicle and if she sees me looking at a non-work-related website, I worry that she will think, "What website is that? Oh some art blog. If I saw Jenny surfing the internet at this moment and since I rarely walk by her desk, Jenny must look at personal websites a lot during

the day. What a slacker! Jenny represents herself as this diligent person. But it's just a façade. She pretends to be hard-working but she's actually a lazy loafer and a faker."

- When I wrote down the above words, I could study the jumps that my mind made from one thought to the next thought. I realized that my paranoia is based on a series of unsubstantiated conclusions. By making my invisible thoughts visible, the thoughts began to lose their power over me.

- I see how the source of perfectionism is shame. I worry that if someone "catches" me in *one* situation of not being perfect, the person will extrapolate this situation as evidence that there is something wrong with me. The belief that something is wrong with me is shame.

Here is another way to view the relationship between perfectionism and shame:

- Shame and the belief that something is wrong with me are both fears.
- Fears become self-fulfilling prophecies.
- Through confirmation bias, I will find evidence that validates that my shame belief is true. I will attribute each less-than-perfect situation as an indication that there is something wrong with me.
- If I didn't believe that something is wrong with me, then I will view each less-than-perfect situation as just a less-than-perfect situation not as a symptom of something else. Without a shame belief, I would understand that imperfection is a natural and inevitable part of living life and of being human.

* * * * *

In each situation, I have the power to decide how I will respond.[8] I can consciously choose the thoughts that I will think instead of just letting myself think the automatic reactive thoughts that arise. Practicing mantras is a way to choose my opinions about situations and about myself. If I repeat a mantra often enough, then the mantra's words will become a way to reprogram my mind to change how I view myself.

Through social conditioning, my mind has created a variety of stimulus-response partnerships in which a specific external stimulus produces corresponding reactive responses. Below is an example:

External stimulus: I look at a website at work.

Reactive response: I have paranoid thoughts, such as "People will think I'm a slacker. People will think I'm a dubious, two-faced person who projects herself as a hard worker but is actually a loafer."

Reactive response: I internalize the uneasy, self-conscious feelings that these thoughts create.

When I notice myself feeling self-conscious and having paranoid thoughts, I can choose new thoughts. I can choose a conscious response to neutralize my reactive response. For example, I can repeat this mantra: "I am a respectable person. People see me as a respectable person. If people see me on the internet right now, they will view this as appropriate behavior because they know that I am a hard worker and that it's natural to take a break."

*   *   *   *   *

Another realization helped to diminish the worry that people are habitually thinking and saying unwelcome things about me: I read somewhere that as conversations evolve, people shift from talking about people to talking about things and ideas. As I've matured and as my relationships have deepened, I've noticed the relevance of this statement in my conversations. As I've gotten older, I talk about ideas more than I talk about things or people. As I get to know a person better, we talk about ideas and things more than we talk about other people. Also, the individuals in my life now are much nicer than the individuals from high school or my first job.

*   *   *   *   *

As I dispel the myths that create my social paranoia, I replace the words *dubious*, *questionable*, and *suspicious* with more favorable character descriptions. To find words for my affirmative mantras, I search the thesaurus and dictionary for adjectives that feel like suitable antonyms for the negative adjectives (or shame labels) that I am purging from my identity.

Trustworthy was one word I found in the thesaurus. It is an antonym for the adjective *suspect*. But the word *trustworthy* felt like a quality a person needs to earn, such as after fulfilling a series of promises.

When I found the word *respectable*, this felt more authentic to me. It felt like a word that I could learn to believe that other people think about me. The word *respectable* felt unconditional, like an attribute that is true about every person. *Respectable* didn't feel like a quality that someone needed to achieve by meeting certain conditions.

*   *   *   *   *

I am not a dubious or questionable person.

I am a respectable person. I am a respectable person. I am a respectable person.

With each affirmation, I am reminding myself I am a golden Buddha.

I am a golden Buddha. I am a golden Buddha. I am a golden Buddha.

Stomach pains

When I call in sick, I worry that my manager and coworkers think that I'm lying and that I'm a slacker who isn't sick.

If I return to work with cold-like symptoms, I feel as if everyone believes that I was honestly sick on my day off. But if I return to work with no symptoms, my inner critics plague me all day long. For example, if I'm sick with nausea, stomach pains, or a mild sore throat, there won't be any lingering visible symptoms for people to observe.

If my manager doesn't ask me how I'm feeling, I imagine it's because she doesn't believe that I was legitimately sick and I worry that she believes that I was taking advantage of having a day off from work.

* * * * *

Why do I worry that people doubt my credibility when I'm not feeling well?

Memory #1: The bed

During my freshman year of college, my boyfriend, Ian, drove four hours to spend Valentine's Day weekend with me. One night, we hiked for a mile through two feet of snow to eat at our favorite Chinese restaurant. Before we left my dorm building, I pulled my coat hood tight against my head so it felt like a second layer of skin. I double knotted the hood's cords to prevent them from unraveling in the wind. Ian didn't have a hood on his jacket. He wore a thick blue and gray striped wool hat that hugged his head like a swimming cap. But at least twice, a gust knocked his hat off and blew it a few feet away from him. When Ian trudged toward his hat and tried to snatch it in the swirling snow, Ian's ears turned pinker and pinker.

On the Monday after Ian left, I was bedridden. My head and body felt like lead. It took so much effort to roll from my back to my side. My legs were so heavy that I needed to inch them toward the edge of my bed to drop my feet to the floor so I could drag myself to the bathroom.

After my roommate returned from class and saw me under the covers, she left the room. She walked up and down the hall shouting into each room with an open door: "Jenny's in bed. She says she's sick. But she's just skipping classes."

Memory #2: The coworker

When I was twenty-eight, I was an internal auditor for a large bank. One of my coworkers, Erica, called in sick often—probably more than anyone else in our department. My coworker, Christine, often said to me, "Whenever Erica comes back to work after calling in sick, she wears her glasses and doesn't wear any makeup. This way, she'll look more tired."

At the time, I felt that Christine was just voicing what everyone else was thinking about Erica's behavior. But now, a decade later, I wonder if anyone else doubted Erica's credibility besides Christine and me (because I believed Christine's theory). Looking back, I realize that Christine had something negative to say about everyone we worked with. At that job, I was touched that Christine wanted to be my friend and that she confided in me. But in hindsight, I realize that Christine was more suspicious, more critical, and less trusting of other people than I was.

If I believe that my current colleagues have Christine's suspicious nature, then it will be easy for me to believe that people think that I'm lying when I call in sick.

*   *   *   *   *

I am not a slacker or a lying person.

I am a conscientious and honest person. I am a conscientious and honest person. I am a conscientious and honest person.

With each affirmation, I am reminding myself I am a golden Buddha.

I am a golden Buddha. I am a golden Buddha. I am a golden Buddha.

*   *   *   *   *

Sometimes my mantras feel awkward to me, especially the initial times that I repeat them. But I know that my mantras have healing powers because I specifically selected each mantra for each trigger situation. Like an antidote for a poison or an immunization for a flu, each mantra contains an affirming adjective derived from the judgmental adjective that I am trying to counteract or to protect against. For example, *honest* is the opposite of *lying* and *conscientious* is an antonym for the word *slack*. When my customized mantras feel phony, I ask myself these two questions:

- How do I want to spend my life?
- What beliefs do I want to fill my mind?

I would rather believe that people think I am a conscientious and honest person than believe that people view me as a slacker and liar.

Three water bottles

I flew to Burbank, California and attended five days of work-related training. The topic was cybersecurity and the conference was held at a Hilton hotel that was a ten minute walk from the Universal Studios theme park.

After I entered my room, I walked around and cleared off all the surfaces. I performed this ritual whenever I stayed in a hotel because I hate clutter and I find it distracting. In the bathroom, I scooped up the plastic bottles of shampoo and lotion, the washcloths, and the bars of soap. I dumped the toiletries into the top dresser drawer. I gathered the hotel pens, notepads, HBO guide, hotel binder, and remote control and put them into the nightstand drawer. I turned the ringers off on the two phones and I set the phones on the carpet under the desk or next to the nightstand.

When I saw three water bottles displayed on the table, I considered shoving them into a drawer too. But the water bottles had $4.00 and $5.00 price tags. Instead, I called the front desk: "Hi, this is room 501. I noticed three water bottles in my room. Will you send someone to my room to take them? Will you also put a note in my record? I don't want the housekeeping staff to charge me or to give me new water bottles whenever they clean my room."

A month after the conference, I got my credit card statement. As I examined it, I saw two amounts from the Hilton: $1,011.20 for my five-night stay and an unknown $16.57 charge.

I called the hotel and spoke with the accountant: "This $16.57 is a mistake. I didn't eat at your hotel's restaurant or order room service."

The accountant said, "It looks like housekeeping entered the $16.57 into the system. It probably relates to the water bottles in the room."

"A man in a gray uniform came to my room to take the bottles away. I had asked the front desk clerk to document a note in my room record. She must have forgotten."

After a few seconds of silence, the accountant said, "I guess I will credit your account for $16.57."

Even though I got what I wanted—a refund of an erroneous charge—the experience made me feel unsettled. I told the truth. But I felt like a liar.

I realized that it was the accountant's tone of voice and his lack of any affirmations that triggered this shame belief in me. For example, if the accountant had said, "That makes sense" or "I understand," I wouldn't have gotten the impression that he thought I was lying. I imagined him thinking, "Who would call to have water bottles removed from her room? I bet she drank all the water and is too cheap to pay. What a cockamamie story! Couldn't she have thought of a more believable explanation? She must think I'm a fool. I guess I have no other alternative than to refund her money."

I replayed the conversation in my mind, thinking of all of the things that I could have said in hopes of having the accountant believe me.

But the problem isn't what I said or didn't say or how I said it. The problem is that I have a tendency to believe that other people think that I'm lying. I recreate this problem over and over again for myself. I seek confirmation from other people of evidence that they believe me. I look for validation of what I said by looking for a positive voice tone in the person's response to me or affirming statements that indicate that the person agrees with my explanation. And when I don't get this validation, I believe the other person thinks I'm lying and I feel something in between uneasiness and inadequacy.

*   *   *   *   *

I am not a liar.

I am an honest and truthful person. I am an honest and truthful person. I am an honest and truthful person.

With each affirmation, I am reminding myself I am a golden Buddha.

I am a golden Buddha. I am a golden Buddha. I am a golden Buddha.

An eraser and a battery tester

Why am I afraid that people think I'm lying and why do I worry that people think I'm a liar? Where did these fears come from?

Two memories stand out in my mind.

<u>Memory #1: The eraser</u>

In second grade, we left our homeroom to have reading class in Mrs. Bailey's classroom. In reading class, we were allowed to choose our own seats. My favorite seat was a corner desk by the door. When I sat in this desk, someone would sit to my right but no one sat to my left. Three feet behind my seat was a white porcelain water fountain, a gray plastic rectangular trash can, and the classroom door. Even as a child, I was efficient and impatient. I didn't like walking across the room for a sip of lukewarm water and I liked to be one of the first students to parade out of the room to our next destination.

After I approached the room, I ran inside and I dropped my books on my coveted desk. My paperback copy of *Amelia Bedelia* and its $3.00 price tag was at the bottom of the stack. On top of my book were the library's hardcover copies of *The Giving Tree* and *Where the Wild Things Are*, two composition notebooks, and my yellow plastic pencil case.

But I had put my books on the desk before the preceding student, Suzy, had finished gathering her pens and pencils from the area.

When I realized this, I picked my stack of books off of the desk and backed away. I waited while Suzy gathered her items and the teacher helped.

However, when I had picked up my books from the desk, I had accidentally picked up Suzy's eraser too. The eraser was a one-inch by two-inch rectangular Papermate Pink Pearl eraser. When the eraser was new, the edges were angled. Each student was given one of these erasers at the beginning of the school year. If you lost your eraser, you needed to ask your parents to buy you a new one. Since the erasers all looked identical, we carved our names into the pink rubber surfaces with black Bic ballpoint pens during lunch break on the first day of school.

When Suzy asked about her eraser, she and the teacher looked inside the desk and on the floor around the desk. Then, I realized that I had the eraser and I gave it to Suzy. With a smile of relief, Suzy thanked me and skipped out of the classroom.

Later that day, our class marched up to the second floor for our weekly music class. At the top of the stairs, Mrs. Bailey was waiting. When she saw me, she said, "Jenny, I want to talk with you."

Since I had been the second student in the line, she and I stood there and watched as twenty-four students passed us. Some students looked at me and then looked up at Mrs. Bailey before they walked through the doorway. Some students were too out of breath to glance over at us. Finally, the last person arrived. After he reached the top of the stairs, he bent over and dropped his hands to his knees to take a break. Then, he jogged through the doorway and down the hall. As soon as we stopped hearing his labored breath and his shuffling feet, Mrs. Bailey put her hands around my shoulders and turned my body to face hers. She didn't squat down so her eyes were level with mine. She stood at her full height of five feet six inches and I needed to tilt my head back to see her face as she spoke.

"Jenny, earlier today, you took Suzy's eraser. When Suzy noticed this, you pretended you didn't realize what you did. I know you were lying and that you were trying to take Suzy's eraser. We do not tolerate lying or stealing."

"Do you understand what I'm saying, Jenny?"

"Yes," I said.

"Good," she replied. Then, she hurried down the stairs.

After a few minutes, I started to walk toward the music room. After I pulled open the door by its brass handle, I stood inside in the mouth of the room. I searched for an empty seat but avoided any eye contact. Then, I walked toward the chairs and squeezed my body in between the chair backs of the second row and the protruding desk surfaces of the chairs of the third row. When I reached the middle of the row, I sat down and opened my music book. I felt weak. My head and shoulders hunched downward. My gaze remained on the sheet music in my book. I didn't have the energy to lift my head to look up at the blackboard as the teacher wrote. All I wanted to do was to fold my arms on my desk, hide my face in that space, and cry.

Memory #2: The battery tester

When I was ten years old, my dad bought a battery tester from Radio Shack. It was a three-inch by three-inch dark gray square plastic contraption. To use it, you raised the "arm" and inserted a battery between the "arm" and a "foot" that protruded from the left side. Since it was cheaply made, sometimes the front of the battery tester separated from the back. Sometimes you could snap the two pieces together and it still worked.

One day, I found the two square pieces scattered on the stairs. The gray pieces stood out against the tan carpet fibers, especially since they were on a step not already occupied by sneakers or flip flops.

I tried to align the two pieces together to return the contraption back to its original condition. It usually took a few seconds. But this time, after a few minutes of effort, the pieces still wouldn't match up.

Since I was in a rush to go to a friend's house, I interrupted a conversation that my parents were having with their friend. I walked over to the oval walnut dining room table and stood next to my dad by the head of the table. My dad was recounting a story. His face contorted into different expressions of surprise and relief as he created shapes in the air with his waving arms.

A man was hunched over a pale yellow plastic bowl decorated with red flowers. A white Bounty paper towel was tucked into the neck of his shirt. In his right hand, he held a pair of black wooden chopsticks. As he inched the white flat pho noodles toward his mouth, his eyes remained locked on my dad's face.

Finally, my dad stopped talking. He didn't say a word to me. He just turned his body in my direction and looked at my face. I gave him the two gray pieces and said, "I found this on the stairs. It was broken when I discovered it. I wanted to give it to you in case you can fix it. I didn't want to leave it on the stairs where it could get stepped on." I didn't wait for my dad to respond. I sped out of the kitchen toward the front door. But as I was leaving the house, I heard my dad say, "Jenny broke it." But he didn't say the words in a compassionate, understanding way. He said them in an accusing way that made me feel as if he thought I had broken it and that I was a liar.

*   *   *   *   *

If I tell the truth and someone blames me for lying, I may begin to believe that people don't trust what I say. If enough people accuse me of being dishonest when I'm honest, then I'll start to believe that people see me as a liar. This is how the accumulation of false accusation after false accusation builds to create the shame label of liar and the social paranoia that people see me as a liar.

Shame source #4:
Decisions and comprehension

Cold medicine

As I stood in Walgreens staring at the shelves of cold medicine, I felt overwhelmed by all of the choices. Do I buy a brand-name or a generic? What is better? Pills, liquid gel tablets, lozenges, or a powder you dissolve in water? Will a throat spray or a cough syrup help Ian sleep better?

After five minutes of reading boxes and bottles, my blue plastic shopping basket remained empty.

I was afraid of making the wrong choice. When I challenged myself to identify the thoughts under my self-doubt, I realized that I was afraid Ian would say, "You got the wrong one. You should have gotten the generic nighttime liquid tablets," or "You should have bought me the sore throat spray," or "You should have brought home some cough drops *without* menthol," or "How could you have been so stupid to have misunderstood me? I should have gone to the store. Now I have the wrong medicine for my runny nose and sore throat and your mistake has cost us time and money."

In the twenty-four years that I've been with Ian, he has never criticized me in this way. And he has never called me stupid. I carried these fears into our relationship and into my present life.

When I looked up the definition for *stupid*, it said: "slow to learn or understand."[9] I see how the adjective *stupid* can be under the surface and can relate to other attributes besides book smarts.

Stupid can describe a person's lack of judgment: "the capacity to assess situations or circumstances and draw sound conclusions."[10] Or *stupid* may mean a lack of comprehension: "the act or fact of grasping the meaning, nature or importance of; understanding."[11]

I realize that I was brought up to distrust my own judgment, comprehension, and decision-making abilities.

*   *   *   *   *

What messages made me doubt my own judgment?

- In high school, I remember getting a bad haircut. The hairdresser was a sweet person who had worked with me at a previous job. I remember my mom's reaction when I came home: "What happened to your hair? I sent you to the mall and this is what happened! Look at all of these hairs that are longer than the rest. She's not even licensed yet. You should have complained and gotten the haircut for free or demanded that someone with more experience fix it. Now I have to pay again to get you another haircut. You tipped her how much??? You are such a fool."

- After getting a coupon for "Free differential oil" in the mail, I brought my car to the dealership to redeem the coupon. My dad wasn't happy when he learned about my mistake: "You got the oil changed? For $35??? I just replaced the oil and oil filter in your car last week! How could you be so dumb?"

- I remember friends saying, "You paid how much for that? You could have gotten that cheaper at T.J. Maxx. You really are clueless," or "Do you know how bad that nail polish is? It contains formaldehyde. If you use that, we'll all have headaches and feel dizzy by the end of the night. We should never have put you in charge of the nail polish for the sleepover. Now we can't paint our nails."

I realize that buying something on behalf of someone else is a situational trigger that makes me feel self-doubt. I worry that the other person will disagree with my decision and will:

- Label my decision as stupid; and
- Extend the label to me as a person and make me feel as if I am stupid for believing that my decision was appropriate.

*   *   *   *   *

My choices are not stupid. I am not simple and clueless.

I make sound decisions.

I am a sensible and judicious person. I am a sensible and judicious person. I am a sensible and judicious person.

With each affirmation, I am reminding myself I am a golden Buddha.

I am a golden Buddha. I am a golden Buddha. I am a golden Buddha.

IF IT'S IMPORTANT TO ME, IT DOESN'T MATTER IF IT'S TRIVIAL TO OTHER PEOPLE.

MY CONCERNS ARE NOT TRIVIAL TO ME. IT'S NOT RIDICULOUS FOR ME TO WORRY ABOUT THE THINGS THAT I WORRY ABOUT.

MY FEELINGS ARE
VALID. I MAKE APPROPRIATE
DECISIONS.

I AM A LEVEL-HEADED
PERSON. I AM A LEVEL-
HEADED PERSON. I AM
A LEVEL-HEADED PERSON.

WITH EACH AFFIRMATION, I AM REMINDING MYSELF THAT I AM A GOLDEN BUDDHA.

I AM A GOLDEN BUDDHA.
I AM A GOLDEN BUDDHA.
I AM A GOLDEN BUDDHA.

I am not responsible for when bad things happen. I am not blameful or inherently culpable.

Sometimes things go wrong & that is life. It isn't necessarily my fault.

I DON'T MAKE UNWISE STUPID DECISIONS. I MAKE PRUDENT CHOICES.

I AM A CAUTIOUS & PRACTICAL PERSON. I AM A CAUTIOUS & PRACTICAL PERSON. I AM A CAUTIOUS & PRACTICAL PERSON.

WITH EACH AFFIRMATION,
I AM REMINDING MYSELF
THAT I AM A GOLDEN
BUDDHA.

I AM A GOLDEN BUDDHA.
I AM A GOLDEN BUDDHA.
I AM A GOLDEN BUDDHA.

IAN THINKS MY SUGGESTION IS ABSURD. IT CLASHES WITH THE DECORATING STYLE OF OUR MAIN FLOOR. LAST YEAR, WE WERE RUTHLESS ABOUT HOW WE REDECORATED OUR HOME. IF AN ART PIECE DIDN'T FIT THE COLOR SCHEME OF A ROOM, THE PIECE WENT TO STORAGE.

ONLY IF YOU ARE OKAY WITH THAT IDEA.

I JUST ASKED, "DO YOU MEAN FOR OUR WALLS?"

WHEN I VOICE AN OPINION, I LOOK FOR AGREEMENT FROM THE OTHER PERSON. WHEN THE OTHER PERSON AGREES WITH ME, THIS VALIDATES THAT MY IDEA HAS VALUE.

WHEN THE OTHER PERSON ASKS ME A QUESTION ABOUT WHAT I JUST SAID, THIS TRIGGERS SELF-DOUBT FOR ME. I INTERPRET QUESTIONS AS EVIDENCE THAT THE OTHER PERSON DISAGREES WITH WHAT I JUST SAID.

MY SUBCONSCIOUS IMAGINES THAT THE QUESTION IS A POLITE WAY OF SAYING, "THAT'S A STUPID IDEA! YOU'RE SO SIMPLE TO BELIEVE THAT YOUR IDEAS ARE WORTHWHILE."

MY IDEAS ARE NOT STUPID & VALUELESS. MY OPINIONS ARE VALID. MY VIEWS HAVE MERIT. I HAVE GREAT IDEAS!

I AM A LOGICAL & RATIONAL PERSON. I AM A LOGICAL & RATIONAL PERSON. I AM A LOGICAL & RATIONAL PERSON.

WITH EACH AFFIRMATION
I AM REMINDING MYSELF
THAT I AM A GOLDEN
BUDDHA.

I AM A GOLDEN BUDDHA.
I AM A GOLDEN BUDDHA.
I AM A GOLDEN BUDDHA.

The restaurant

IT'S EASIER TO IDENTIFY WHAT I WANT WHEN I AM BY MYSELF THAN WHEN SOMEONE ELSE IS INVOLVED. WHEN I TOLD MY FRIEND, JUSTIN, ABOUT THIS INSIGHT, HE TOLD ME ABOUT A CONVERSATION HE HAD WITH HIS HUSBAND, RICHARD.

THIS COMIC DEPICTS TWO CONVERSATIONS.

A FEW WEEKS LATER, CONVERSATION #2 BETWEEN JUSTIN & JENNY.

JENNY, WHEN RICHARD ASKED ME WHERE I WANTED TO GO TO DINNER, I WAS CRAVING, CRAVING ENCHILADAS.

I COULD TASTE THE CHEESE, THE SPANISH RICE, THE REFRIED BEANS.

JUSTIN, I KNOW WHAT YOU MEAN. WHENEVER IAN ASKS "WHAT DO YOU WANT TO DO TONIGHT?" OR "WHAT MOVIE DO YOU WANT TO SEE?" I CHOOSE WHAT I THINK IAN WANTS.

ACTUALLY, I DO THIS ALL THE TIME. I AM NOT EVEN AWARE OF IT. I GUESS WHAT THE OTHER PERSON WANTS INSTEAD OF THINKING ABOUT WHAT I TRULY WANT.

Shame source #5:

Making requests

The treasure chests

At an art workshop, the teacher explained the project and the available supplies: "You will each decorate a set of three nested boxes that will represent your public self, private self, and secret self. I have a variety of brown paper maché box shapes for you to choose from. There are a lot of nested squares, ovals, and circles. There are two sets each of the boxes that look like a book, heart, and treasure chest. I also have some tiny one-inch octagonal boxes if you want to put them inside your smallest nested box. You can decorate your paper maché boxes with whatever supplies you see on and under these three tables."

When the teacher held up the treasure chest box, my eyes widened. That shape called to me! Since I wanted that box so much I felt as if everyone else wanted it too. I worried about how there were only two sets of treasure chest boxes and twelve students in class. After the teacher ended her explanations, we all walked up to the tables to choose our boxes. I hovered by the treasure chest boxes for a minute. Since no one had picked them up, I felt safe to choose a set for myself.

After I gathered my supplies, I waited to paint my treasure chest boxes until after each student had started to work on her boxes. As I turned my head and shoulders around and surveyed the room, I noticed that no one else had selected the other set of treasure chests. In that moment, I decided that I would begin to trust my wants and to worry less about whether my actions denied someone else from something that she wanted.

After three hours of decorating our boxes, we prepared for our show and tell time. We cleared off the tables in the center of the room and lined up our nested boxes. We displayed the lids separately from the boxes to make it easier for others to see how we decorated the insides of the boxes.

Inside my smallest treasure chest box, I had the following items:

- A one-inch octagonal box with twenty plastic googly eyes. The eyes symbolized how most of my inner critics arose when I was with other people, and the inner criticisms related to how I should have behaved.
- A one-inch octagonal box of plastic skulls. The skulls represented how I carried unhelpful beliefs from my childhood, and I needed to bury these beliefs.
- Four half-inch plastic lanterns that reminded me to make my invisible social conditioning and inner criticisms visible. When I was aware of them, I stopped letting them control what I thought.

Since we were busy walking around looking at each other's creations, we interpreted each piece on our own rather than hearing the artist explain what each decorative element meant to her.

As we packed away our boxes to head home, I overheard my teacher say, "took all of my eyeballs."

Since I was the only student who had used eyeballs in her piece, my paranoid self told me, "She's talking about you, Jenny!!!" Tears welled up in the outside corners of my eyes. Mixed with shame, I also felt confusion and anger. I pictured the $350 check that I wrote for the art workshop. I also visualized the quart-sized plastic tub that still held over two cups of googly eyes. During the workshop, I had thought that my $350 payment allowed me access to whatever supplies I wanted to use. But was this belief wrong?

That night, I wrote about the experience. What was I afraid of during the arts and crafts activity? What was I worried that people would think of me? *Greedy* and *selfish* were the words that arose.

*   *   *   *   *

I pieced together these social rules from my mom. They relate to whenever I am a guest at a get together:

- Don't choose something that someone else may want.
- Even if the hostess says to help yourself, only take a small helping.
- If you deny someone something she wants or if someone thinks that you took too much, people will view you as greedy and selfish. Then, people will badmouth you to others, and with these labels, you won't be invited to future gatherings.

I was brought up to play the role of the subordinate guest. I was taught to view myself and my wishes as inferior to other people and to what they may want.

*   *   *   *   *

I am not greedy or selfish.

I am thoughtful and mindful. I am thoughtful and mindful. I am thoughtful and mindful.

With each affirmation, I am reminding myself I am a golden Buddha.

I am a golden Buddha. I am a golden Buddha. I am a golden Buddha.

WHEN I THINK ABOUT THIS SITUATION, I REALIZE THAT I USUALLY FEEL UNEASY MAKING REQUESTS OF OTHER PEOPLE. WHETHER IT'S FOR A PHYSICAL OBJECT OR IT'S FOR THEIR TIME & ENERGY FOR THEM TO DO SOMETHING FOR ME.

PART OF IT RELATES TO WORTH. WHEN I MAKE A REQUEST, I WORRY THAT THE PERSON IS THINKING, "WHAT HAVE YOU GIVEN ME TO MAKE THIS REQUEST OF ME?" OR "WHO DO YOU THINK YOU ARE TO IMPOSE ON ME?"

WHERE DID THIS DISBELIEF OF PEOPLE'S AGREEMENTS TO MY REQUESTS COME FROM? I HAVE VAGUE MEMORIES OF MY MOM & HER FRIENDS COMPLAINING TO EACH OTHER ABOUT THINGS THEY SAID YES TO BUT RESENTED EVEN BEING ASKED.

IF a PERSON says yes,
I WILL BELIeve THat SHE IS
COMFORTABLE WITH
MY REQUEST.

MY REQUESTS aRE NOT
PRESUMPTUOUS. I am NOT a
PUSHY OR FORWARD
PERSON.

MY REQUESTS ARE VALID &
APPROPRIATE. I AM ATTENTIVE
TO PEOPLE'S TIME & CONCERNS.

I AM A REASONABLE &
RESPECTFUL PERSON. I AM A
REASONABLE & RESPECTFUL
PERSON. I AM A REASONABLE
& RESPECTFUL PERSON.

WITH EACH AFFIRMATION,
I AM REMINDING MYSELF
THAT I AM A GOLDEN
BUDDHA.

I AM A GOLDEN BUDDHA.
I AM A GOLDEN BUDDHA.
I AM A GOLDEN BUDDHA.

Emails and meeting invitations

I'm an auditor for a bank. To perform my job, I need to review documents and conduct interviews. This involves emailing colleagues to request that they pull documents for me and sending meeting invitations to interview department managers.

Sending email requests and meeting invitations triggers feelings of self-consciousness and self-doubt for me. When I analyzed the timeline of my actions and thoughts, I realized that I add these unhappy feelings to my life.

10 A.M.: I email a request for documents or I send a meeting invitation to a colleague.

10 A.M. – 12 P.M.: While I wait for my colleague to acknowledge my request or meeting invitation, I fill this time up with self-doubt and self-criticism. I feel uneasy. Each time I see the envelope icon in my Microsoft Outlook toolbar indicating that I got an email, I worry that it's a person writing one of the following comments to me:

- It's unreasonable of you to want this information by your timeframe. I have a lot of projects going on right now. How do you not understand that?
- Who do you think you are to want this information by that date?

- You sent your meeting invitation at 10 A.M. today. You want to meet at 9 A.M. tomorrow? It's a common courtesy to give at least 24 hours' notice for a meeting.

12 P.M.: When the person emails me or accepts my meeting invitation and doesn't criticize me, I feel validated. I then realize that she doesn't see anything inappropriate with my request or that at least she doesn't feel strongly enough to voice any concerns.

* * * * *

Why do I live in fear of being criticized?

I can't remember the last time a colleague criticized me by email. Yet, I allow myself to repeat this cycle of worrying over and over again.

* * * * *

Why do I delay my inner peace until I get external validation?

10 A.M.: I send the email.
10 A.M. – 12 P.M.: I worry.
12 P.M.: My colleague responds with no criticism. I feel validated.

* * * * *

Why don't I self-validate myself right away?

Then, I can fill the waiting time with confidence instead of worry.

10 A.M.: I send the email. I validate myself by thinking thoughts, such as "I am a reasonable person. I need this information to do my job and I also have a deadline to meet. They will understand this. If people don't understand and lash out at me, their criticisms will be reflections of their stress, not of me as a person."

10 A.M. – 12 P.M.: I feel confidence and inner peace.

12 P.M.: I get my colleague's response and no criticism.

*   *   *   *   *

My requests for documents are not overbearing. My invitations for meetings are not discourteous.

My document requests and meeting invitations are fair and appropriate.

I am not an unreasonable and overbearing person.

I am a reasonable and thoughtful person. I am a reasonable and thoughtful person. I am a reasonable and thoughtful person.

With each affirmation, I am reminding myself I am a golden Buddha.

I am a golden Buddha. I am a golden Buddha. I am a golden Buddha.

The phone call

Once I emailed a colleague a question. Two weeks later, I needed to know her answer. So I decided to call her. I dislike calling people because phone calls carry an inherent urgency. When I examined my reluctance, I identified what I was afraid my colleague would think:

- Ugggh. Why is Jenny calling me? Phone calls are so disruptive. Jenny could have emailed me. *(I was worried that my colleague would judge my action as inappropriate.)*
- Jenny wants to know what? That is so meaningless. I have to deal with more important things than that. *(I was worried that my colleague would judge the reason that prompted my phone call.)*
- Jenny is so bothersome. Jenny is such a bother. *(I was worried that my colleague would judge me as a person.)*

When I studied my list of paranoid thoughts, I identified this hierarchy of negative adjectives:

Reading the words *bothersome* and *bother* clarified something for me. Whenever I make a request of someone, I worry about being bothersome. This is because I associate adjectives, such as *disruptive* or *meaningless*, as indications that I, as a person, am bothersome. I was brought up believing that I am a bother and that I bother people with my unreasonable requests.

*   *   *   *   *

My requests are not meaningless or bothersome.

My approach to making my requests is thoughtful.

My requests are reasonable and necessary.

I am a fair and accommodating person. I am a fair and accommodating person. I am a fair and accommodating person.

With each affirmation, I am reminding myself I am a golden Buddha.

I am a golden Buddha. I am a golden Buddha. I am a golden Buddha.

Shame source #6:
Being courteous

The circus

Recently, I flew to Baltimore, Maryland for the weekend to visit my sister, Jackie, and her sons. Jackie bought tickets for everyone in our family to see the Ringling Bros. and Barnum & Bailey Circus.

"Did we go to the circus as kids?" Jackie asked. "I have no memory of it. We must have gone. Anyways, it will be fun to take JD and Joshua. JD loves elephants. I'm excited to see how they react to the acrobats and the clowns."

When we arrived at the stadium that housed the circus, my family split up. My brother-in-law and youngest brother waited outside for my other brother. My sister brought her four-year-old to a concession stand to look at the toys and food. My mom and I took the one-year-old to sit down.

When we arrived at our seats, we found an elderly couple and a ten-year-old sitting in between them. "Hi," I said. "It looks like you're sitting in our seats."

"Are you sure?" the man asked before he scooped his hand into a red and white striped bag of popcorn.

"Yes, we're in section 324, row S, seats 10 through 18."

The man shifted his weight to his right side, reached his left hand behind him and pulled out his ticket. He held the ticket two inches from his eyes and read, "Section 323, row S, seat 15."

I pointed to the wall ten feet behind us. In large black paint was the number 324. The man grabbed the right armrest with his left hand and turned his shoulders and head to look behind him. Then he turned his head to the left and to the right. "322, 326," he said. "Where is 323?"

"On the other side. This part of the stadium contains the even-numbered sections. The other side is odd-numbered."

"Oh okay. It will take a moment for us to gather our things."

I looked down at the seat next to the man and saw a stack of black wool trench coats and a cream scarf and a blue scarf centered exactly in the middle of the black rectangular shape. The man's wife and grandson each also had a two-gallon-sized bag of popcorn. I saw three of the 64-ounce special edition reusable plastic soda cups that I had seen earlier at the concession stand.

The man leaned forward and yelled, "Charlie, we need to move."

I turned around and whispered to my mom, "Let's wait in the aisle."

To prepare for the couple's exit, we stood on the concrete step above our row. As we waited, my eyes darted between observing the couple's progress and scrutinizing the people walking up the stairs toward us. As the couple put on their coats and scarves and bent over to collect their belongings, my feeling of self-consciousness grew and grew. I worried about being in someone's way.

Then I heard a voice behind me say, "Excuse me."

I turned around and saw a man with a two-year-old girl sitting on his shoulders. Behind the man was a woman hugging a group of puffy down jackets.

In those two little words, "Excuse me," I felt like a rude little girl who had gotten in his way and had inconvenienced him and his family. Shame washed over me. My whole body heated up and my armpits began sweating.

*   *   *   *   *

When I examined this situation, I realized that subtle things, such as the tone of a voice and the length of a comment, can feel like disapproval or approval to me of my preceding behavior. The man's short remark and his neutral tone of voice triggered the physical feeling of shame in me.

What if the man had used a friendlier upbeat voice?

What if he had said more words, such as "Excuse me. You happen to be standing in front of the same row we want to enter"?

I would have been unaffected by him.

*   *   *   *   *

I realize that I am like one of Pavlov's dogs who was trained to salivate at the sound of a bell. I am a subject of social conditioning.

At one time in my life, a neutral, stern, or raised voice and the use of minimal words may have held no meaning to me. But after they were the ways that someone reproached me, I began to associate them with the belief and feeling that I had done something wrong.

Social conditioning created the below stimulus-response relationship in my mind:

- Conditioned stimuli: Minimal words and any voice tone that is less than cheery.
- Conditioned response - subconscious thoughts: I did something wrong and something is wrong with me.

- Conditioned response - physiological reaction in which I feel shame:
  - Tears well up in the outside corners of my eyes, my head bends down slightly, and my throat tightens up as if my body is preparing to cry and also choke back the tears; or
  - My breath speeds up, and my heart beats quickly and sporadically in my chest as if my body is engaged in running away from what I'm afraid of; or
  - My face and chest heat up and my armpits get moist.

Now as an adult, even though I'm not being criticized for something, a tone of voice accompanied with a terse sentence evokes a physiological feeling of shame in me.

But if I am aware of this stimulus-response relationship, then I can choose conscious thoughts to neutralize my conditioned response. (My conditioned responses are shaming thoughts that tell me that I did something wrong and that something is wrong with me.) I can instead think, "Oh. He was concise and his voice was neutral or raised. These are conditioned stimuli that trigger shame for me. I didn't do anything wrong. There is nothing wrong with me."

*   *   *   *   *

I am not a rude person.

I am an attentive and mindful person. I am an attentive and mindful person. I am an attentive and mindful person.

With each affirmation, I am reminding myself I am a golden Buddha.

I am a golden Buddha. I am a golden Buddha. I am a golden Buddha.

The four-year-old

Later that year, in September, I took another redeye flight from Seattle to Baltimore to visit my sister and nephews. This time, I stayed for three days instead of two. Exhausted from the redeye, I took a nap every day that weekend. I usually napped when my nephews napped.

By the third day, I was mentally exhausted and homesick. That day, when I woke up from my nap, I noticed my four-year-old nephew sitting on the carpet next to my bed. He was playing with a wooden Buddha statue, a small jewelry box, my hair scrunchie, and my pen from the nightstand.

When I saw him, I didn't say, "It was sweet of you to want to be near me," or "Hi JD. What are you doing?" or "Thank you for being so good and quiet while I slept."

Instead, I jumped out of bed and shooed him out of the room and yelled, "Let me have my privacy! This is my room!" Then, I locked the door and crawled back under the covers.

*   *   *   *   *

When I looked back over the weekend, I recalled a few times when my sister scolded JD for something he did or didn't do:

- What are you doing roaming around? You're supposed to be napping. *If you miss your nap, you'll be cranky later. I can't handle that today.*
- Put on your cleats! You can either play soccer in your socks or your cleats or we're going home! This is the last time I'm telling you! *Don't make us later than we already are.*
- How many of those bags did you open? Don't touch what isn't yours! Go to time-out for five minutes! *I better have enough bags for tomorrow's party!*

When I think about my nap and the above situations, I see a similarity in the criticisms. In each moment, the adult wanted something and the four-year-old was denying the adult from what she wanted or putting what she wanted at risk. For me, it was privacy. For my sister, it was peace, timeliness, order, and confidence.

There were probably a dozen more instances of someone criticizing JD that weekend. There were also many times when my sister complimented JD's behavior or appreciated him as a person:

- Thank you JD for asking us so nicely.
- It made me happy that you waited until we stopped talking before you asked us your questions. That was very polite of you.
- I appreciated how you said thank you, please, and excuse me at dinner.
- You did a really good job at listening to Nana, Daddy, and me today.
- Thank you for sharing with Joshua this afternoon. You're such a loving and nice big brother.
- JD, you're a really good boy.

JD is a good kid and Jackie is a loving and attentive parent. My sister is conscientious about how she raises her children. She has the self-awareness, time, and energy to remind JD what a well-behaved person he is. Jackie's frequent affirming messages will neutralize the criticisms that JD receives in his life.

*   *   *   *   *

For me, as a child, the criticisms from my parents and other adults accumulated to create a belief that I am an inconsiderate person who does things that upset other people or who fails to do what I'm supposed to do:

- What are you doing out here? Can't you tell I'm trying to sleep? Go outside!
- Split your candy bar with your sister! If you didn't want to share, you should have eaten it in secret. It's your fault that she's whining.
- Stop letting flies into the house! Shut the screen door after you leave! If it's open an inch, that's a whole inch that bugs can get in!
- Who ate the last of the ice cream?!?!?!
- There's only a few tablespoons of milk left. Why did you put the carton back in the fridge?
- Slowpoke! Hurry up! What's taking you so long?
- I'm busy right now. Go away!
- Turn out the lights! I'm not made of money!
- Stop drinking so much! We're already late and I don't have time to pull over at a gas station.

I heard these types of criticisms a lot. But I didn't receive compliments about my behavior and I wasn't told that I was a good or well-behaved child. With the abundance of criticisms and the lack of affirmations, I internalized the belief that I am an inconsiderate person who inconveniences and irritates other people.

*   *   *   *   *

I am not an inconsiderate person who irritates other people.

I am a considerate and conscientious person. I am a considerate and conscientious person. I am a considerate and conscientious person.

With each affirmation, I am reminding myself I am a golden Buddha.

I am a golden Buddha. I am a golden Buddha. I am a golden Buddha.

The concert stadium

After I left the restroom, I walked toward the stadium section where my seat was. It was challenging to weave my way between the people lined up to buy food, the people walking in my same direction, and the people walking toward me.

As I approached a booth selling concert T-shirts, it became more congested. As I squeezed by people, I started to get up-close views of plastic cups filled with beer. The amber liquids sloshed just below the mouths of their open containers.

I worried about people spilling their drinks on me. If a person didn't stop in time and slammed her cup against my chest, it wouldn't hurt. But the beer would soak through my two shirts and make my skin and bra wet. My shirts would be damp and sticky for hours and I'd worry about a stain developing in the center of my favorite shirt.

When I thought about my possible reactions, I discovered four levels of communication:

1. That's okay. I've done that before. *(Level 1 communication expresses empathy.)*
2. That's okay. It happens. *(Level 2 communication expresses understanding.)*
3. Look what you did! *(Level 3 communication judges the behavior.)*
4. You're such an idiot! *(Level 4 communication judges the person.)*

With level 4 communication, I may not even say the word "idiot." But the tone of my voice, facial expressions, or body language may imply that I'm judging the person.

Level 3 and 4 communications convey that the person did something wrong. Level 1 and 2 communications convey that the person didn't do anything wrong; what happened was an honest mistake and a natural part of life.

My level of communication in that moment and in other moments would have been heavily influenced by my energy level or mood. If I was already feeling impatient or I was currently stressed and overwhelmed, I would most likely have lashed out with level 3 or 4 communication.

When I am calm or relaxed, I tend to respond with level 1 or 2 communication. When I am irritable, everything and everyone irritates me. When I am happy, I am more easy-going and more forgiving of things that happen.

*　　*　　*　　*　　*

I see now that my parents were mostly stuck in survival mode. They were just trying to make it through each day. As a result, they were continually stuck in stress mode or irritability mode and often chastised me with level 3 or 4 communication.

If my parents had been self-aware enough of their actions, they would have later told me, "When I yelled at you earlier, it wasn't you—it was me. I was feeling tense and anything would have made me angry at that moment. And in that moment, it happened to be you."

But my parents and the other adults in my past never pulled me aside to explain or apologize for their outbursts toward me. They didn't say any of the following explanations to me:

- I recognize that you were trying to keep your voice down while I slept. These walls are thinner than we realize.

- I know that you bought your candy with your allowance and it's not much fun to share. I didn't have the patience to explain this to your sister. So I made you give her some of your Snickers bar to quiet her.

- I love the summer. But I hate the flies. With six people in the family and all of your friends and your siblings' friends coming in and out of the house, that's a lot of opportunities for more flies to get into our house. We all need to make an extra effort to check that the screen door closes tightly against the door frame.

- You didn't do anything wrong by eating the ice cream. I bought it for all of us to eat. I was just looking forward to it. I was disappointed when I discovered that it was gone. I could have driven to the store to buy more but I was too tired.

- When you put a container back into the fridge and there's less than a serving size in it, it's misleading to me when I make the grocery list. I don't know that I should buy more of it.

- I'm sorry that I called you a slowpoke yesterday. I was feeling anxious about the traffic and getting to Mr. Tucker's house. I wanted to make a good impression by being on time.

- Jenny, thank you for waiting. What did you want to talk with me about? When you last saw me, I was concentrating on something. I was trying to figure out why the stereo wasn't working and it was stressing me out.

- I understand that you're conscientious about turning off the lights when you leave a room. I'm tense now because the utility and credit card bills arrived today and they were much higher than I was expecting. That is why I yelled at you today.

- I know I'm always advocating, "Drink more water." When we have a long car ride, it's good to drink less beforehand. If we all do this, we can make the drive more efficient.

Since my parents didn't tell me things like the previously listed clarifications, they didn't turn their earlier level 3 and 4 yelling into level 1 or 2 communications. As a result, with the accumulation of level 3 and 4 messages, it was easy for my younger self to conclude that I was a discourteous person who frustrated people.

*   *   *   *   *

I am not a discourteous person.

I am a considerate person. I am a considerate person. I am a considerate person.

With each affirmation, I am reminding myself I am a golden Buddha.

I am a golden Buddha. I am a golden Buddha. I am a golden Buddha.

Shame source #7:
Being helpful

The Coke bottle

On our last day in London, Ian and I walked along Portobello Road. Sometimes we'd walk into a store and look around. Sometimes I'd press my face an inch away from the window and peer inside the store and say, "No. Nothing interesting." At the top of the hill, I saw a natural food store. "Tea!" I yelled. "I want to see if they have Pukka Three Ginger Tea!" I ran into the store and found the orange boxes that I was looking for. I scooped up four boxes and cradled them against my chest with my right forearm and walked to the cash register.

After I left the store, I found Ian standing on the sidewalk. He was balancing his Canon digital SLR camera and his open backpack.

"What are you doing?" I asked.

"Trying to find my Coke," Ian said.

"Would you like me to hold your camera?"

"No."

I watched as Ian grasped the lens of his camera with his left thumb, pointer finger, and middle finger. His ring finger and pinky finger created a hook shape that held the strap of his backpack.

As he dug his right hand into his bag, he tilted his head up toward the sky. As he darted his hand around the interior and felt each item, I could see him thinking, "No. No. No," as he touched each item that wasn't his drink. I pictured him touching the Lonely Planet London book, his extra camera lenses, and his umbrella.

"Maybe you could rest your bag on this bench," I said.

"I'm fine."

After a minute, I wanted to ask, "Can I hold your backpack for you?" I didn't. I realized that underneath my suggestion was a fear that Ian would drop him camera and it would be my fault.

Since Ian would never accuse me of this, I wanted to understand the source of my worries and my insistence to help.

In my self-inquiry, I realized that I was worried that Ian would yell, "Can't you see how much I'm doing? And all you do is just stand there? You didn't even offer to help! How can you be so self-absorbed?"

If I asked only once to help, I worried Ian would snap, "Are you blind? Can't you see that things got worse? You should have asked again if you could help!"

Or, if I made more than two suggestions, I was afraid that Ian would shout, "Stop your nagging. I already told you I have it under control."

I couldn't identify any specific memories of when someone said these things to me in my past. But I know these accusations were screamed to me often enough that the words got recorded in my mind as shame tapes. In certain situations, my subconscious mind replays these shame tapes to remind me that I am a bad person because I'm not helpful enough.

I realize that I believe the following:

- If something bad happens, it is my fault. I am to blame.
- I am responsible for anticipating and attending to other people's needs. If I don't, I'm self-absorbed and thoughtless.

*　　*　　*　　*　　*

I am not a self-absorbed and thoughtless person.

I am an attentive and mindful person. I am an attentive and mindful person. I am an attentive and mindful person.

With each affirmation, I am reminding myself I am a golden Buddha.

I am a golden Buddha. I am a golden Buddha. I am a golden Buddha.

The complaint

I have two competing objectives in my mind:

1. The desire to meet other people's needs, such as to be helpful
2. The desire to protect my time and positive energy

For example, a coworker asked me for advice about a problem that she was having. After she explained the situation, I offered her my suggestions about what to do. But she continued to tell me about her situation. This felt like complaining to me instead of necessary background information to help me give her advice. So, I started to exit the conversation.

Setting boundaries is hard for me because I leave conversations feeling uneasy and inadequate. I replay the discussion in my mind and ask myself repeatedly, "Was I helpful enough?"

*   Was I helpful enough?
    I didn't stay and listen to her repeat the details of the situation to me and recount the different reasons why the circumstances were unfair.

*   Was I helpful enough?
    I listened to her background story and gave her thoughtful advice. I'm not sure if she'll do what I recommended.

- Was I helpful enough?
  She gave me a halfhearted response: "Thank you for your time." She didn't thank me for my advice. Maybe she found it unhelpful. She didn't thank me for listening. I was in that room for over thirty minutes. How much time would I need to spend for her to feel listened to?

From this situation, I learned the following about myself:

- I aim to be helpful. If I feel that I am helpful, I feel useful and worthy. If I don't feel that I am helpful, I worry that the other person views my action and me as indifferent, uncaring, and selfish.
- I derive my sense of worth from being helpful and I want people to see me as helpful. As a result, when other people don't make me feel that I am helpful to them, I feel unworthy.

＊　＊　＊　＊　＊

I am not an indifferent and uncaring person.

I am a caring person who practices self-care and mindful actions.

I am a caring and compassionate person. I am a caring and compassionate person. I am a caring and compassionate person.

With each affirmation, I am reminding myself I am a golden Buddha.

I am a golden Buddha. I am a golden Buddha. I am a golden Buddha.

Shame source #8:
My social and economic background

Bare feet

My parents didn't have college degrees. My dad and mom didn't work in offices. My dad worked in a large printing shop. For many years, my mom worked in a factory putting Twizzlers or RCA VCRs into cardboard boxes. But because my parents had less money and less education than other people in our community, there was a stigma that we also knew less about how we were supposed to act. This was also coupled with how my parents were immigrants to the United States.

As a child, adults and peers constantly criticized me about how to behave and what to say and what not to say.

- You don't say, "I went to the bathroom." You say, "I visited the ladies' room."
- You don't say, "I just pooped." You say, "I had a bowel movement." Or, you just don't talk about it.
- You don't put your elbows on the dinner table.
- You don't ask adults how old they are.

Yes, it was normal for a kid to be unaware of an appropriate way to behave until it was explained to her. But I didn't feel that way when I received this feedback. I felt as if there was something wrong with me for not knowing these things yet. I also felt that there was something wrong with my parents because they had not pointed out and corrected my behavior before my criticizers did.

Sometimes the adults and peers began their advice with words such as "Here in America, we…" or "I was *taught* that you shouldn't…" Even when their suggestions didn't begin with these phrases, I still sensed that their admonitions implied that I was lower class than them. I felt their belief of superiority over me.

* * * * *

One sunny May day in Minneapolis before a Twins game, I realized that I feel shame about my social and economic background.

I was sitting in the bleachers waiting for the baseball game to begin. Since our section was empty, I rested my bare feet on the seat in front of me. But I felt self-conscious. I worried that someone would shout, "Put your shoes on. That's disgusting! This isn't your home. This is a public place!"

I was afraid that anyone who saw me and my bare feet would think I was this ignorant, uncivilized person who committed some sort of social impropriety.

In this moment of uneasiness, I recognized that when I'm in public, I continually doubt myself. I constantly wonder if I'll do or say something that someone will judge as ignorant, backward, or indecent.

As I gazed at the green landscape of the empty baseball field, I remembered two memories of when I felt accused of being socially uneducated:

- I was at Barnes & Noble reading a book. I was sitting in an armchair with my legs crossed and my flip flops on the floor in front of the chair. An employee came by and said, "Put your shoes on!!!!" When the woman said these words to me, I felt shame wash over me. My face and body got hot and red. Even though the woman looked to be my age, her direct

135

words and stern face made me feel like I was a bad child who had done something indecent and shameful.

- I also felt this same feeling of ignorance and shame when I was at a Borders bookstore. I was sitting on the carpet in front of a shelf of books. An employee walked by and said, "There's no sitting allowed!!!!"

These were such short memories and when did they occur? Probably ten years ago.

These situations had a strong effect on me because I believe that if a person judges my behavior as inappropriate or disgusting, then the person is also judging me as an ignorant and low-class person. My mind reaches this conclusion because I have this hierarchy of negative adjectives ingrained in my mind:

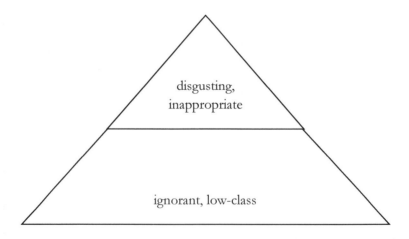

This hierarchy of negative adjectives is why I tend to feel self-conscious when I'm in public.

*   *   *   *   *

Ten years from now, do I want to feel trapped by self-doubt and self-conscious worries about breaking some social decorum or some rule on a list of appropriate manners? Or, do I want to feel self-assurance and inner peace?

My future depends on whether I continue to ignore the shame label that I am a socially ignorant person or if I address and reject this shame label from my subconscious identity.

*   *   *   *   *

If someone disagrees with my behavior or judges it, it is her opinion. It is not a reflection of me.

I am not an ignorant, low-class person who has improper behavior.

I am a self-aware person who has appropriate manners.

I am a self-aware and appropriate person. I am a self-aware and appropriate person. I am a self-aware and appropriate person.

With each affirmation, I am reminding myself I am a golden Buddha.

I am a golden Buddha. I am a golden Buddha. I am a golden Buddha.

Childhood home

When I was six, my family moved to the suburbs. My parents bought a house in a neighborhood where there were two styles of houses and five colors of siding to choose from.

Our home was a split-level house in which the front door opened up to the area containing the stairs. The stairs to the right led up to the main floor and the stairs to the left brought you down to the basement. The house was 1600 square feet. It had three bedrooms and one and a half bathrooms for the six of us in my family.

My parents were very proud to own their first home. I was very proud too.

But in high school, I started to become ashamed of my house. I made friends with girls who lived in other neighborhoods. My new friends had homes that were two or three times bigger than mine. Their houses were always clean. Every room smelled of vanilla or cinnamon. All the towels in their bathrooms matched and looked new.

My house smelled of grease and kerosene. The kitchen sink was continually filled with dirty plates and stacks of macaroni-and-cheese-encrusted pots. Piles of used, frayed towels lay on the bathroom floor. The carpet had groups of individual carpet fibers that had clumped together with accumulated dirt.

*　　*　　*　　*　　*

When I was eighteen, I began attending a private liberal arts college that was ten minutes away from my house. During my four years there, I never invited any of my college friends to my house.

*　　*　　*　　*　　*

I remember when my sister, Jackie, got married at age twenty-six. Before her wedding, she hosted a party in the backyard of our childhood home. Beforehand, she obsessed about cleaning the house. This included parking a dumpster in the driveway and filling the container with things she found in the house. I remember my brother saying, "Jackie, you don't have to worry. Everyone coming to your wedding knows where you came from."

*　　*　　*　　*　　*

As a child and preteen, I was proud of my house and I found its cluttered, aging, and stained nature acceptable. My parents each worked two jobs and the state of our house was a byproduct of how they were rarely home. But as I got exposed to more houses and other ways that people lived, these comparisons turned my satisfaction into shame.

My childhood home and what it looked like inside became clues that my family had less money, less sophistication, and less emphasis on cleaning. The differences between my life and my classmates' lives made me feel substandard.

*　　*　　*　　*　　*

After I moved out of my parents' house, I focused on improving myself. I subconsciously escaped my sense of inferiority by accomplishing goals. Sometimes the goals had short durations, such as preparing for and obsessing about what I'd say in a conversation or meeting. Sometimes the goals had longer time frames, such as revamping my wardrobe, earning my CPA, or attending communication skills classes every year.

Throughout my adult life, I strove to talk and act perfectly. I aimed to present myself as a polished, educated person. But to me, these accomplishments were costumes to hide the *real* me from the world.

Under the successes, I was afraid that people would see where I came from or my less-than background. I was afraid that people would see me as shady, lazy, stupid, inconsiderate, ignorant, and unworthy.

*   *   *   *   *

The secret to self-appreciation and self-love is to just sit with who I am and to address each self-fear with a custom affirmation. The secret is not to run around trying to act perfectly.

This realization reminded me of this Taoist fable:

> There was a man who was so disturbed by the sight of his own shadow and so displeased with his own footsteps that he resolved to get rid of both. The method he hit upon was to run away from them. So he got up and ran. But every time he put his foot down there was another step, while his shadow kept up with him without the slightest difficulty. He attributed his failure to the fact that he was not running fast enough. So he ran faster and faster, without stopping, until he finally dropped dead. He failed to realize that if he merely stepped into the shade, his shadow would vanish, and if he sat down and stayed still, there would be no more footsteps.
>
> -   Chuang Tzu, Taoist philosopher

*   *   *   *   *

The real me is not a less-than person.

The real me is not the shame labels that the people from my past made me believe are truths about me.

The real me is not a shady, lazy, stupid, inconsiderate, ignorant, and unworthy person.

* * * * *

The real me is enough. The real me is more than enough.

The real me is an honest, diligent, smart, considerate, and appropriate person.

The real me is a whole, virtuous, and worthy person.

* * * * *

With each affirmation, I am reminding myself I am a golden Buddha.

I am a golden Buddha. I am a golden Buddha. I am a golden Buddha.

You can search throughout the

entire universe for someone who is

more deserving of your love and

affection than you are yourself, and

that person is not to be found

anywhere. You, yourself, as much as

anybody in the entire universe,

deserve your love and affection.

- Buddha

Gratitude

Many people have helped me become the person I am today and have helped me create a life filled with so much inner peace and contentment.

- Thank you Ian for your love and support. You make me so happy.
- Thank you to my mom and dad for doing the best job you could in raising me and for all of the sacrifices that you made to give me opportunities in life.
- Thank you to John, Jackie, and James for your love. I love you all very much.
- Thank you to my yoga teachers for empowering me with the skills of self-awareness. A special thank you goes out to Molly Lannon Kenny, Stephanie Sisson, Megan Carroll, Laura Humpf, and Veronica Waters Beck.
- Thank you to all my art and writing teachers for helping me to find my voice.
- Thank you to every author who has written a self-help book. Your wisdom has changed my life.
- Thank you to my friends for your love, acceptance, and appreciation and for helping me to see the value in sharing my art and writing with other people.

About the author

When I was six years old, I knew that I would become a writer and that I would write a book. I made this decision after receiving my first rejection letter.

I had entered a writing contest sponsored by my elementary school. I don't remember the theme or the guidelines for the submissions. I only remember that I created a Pac-Man comic as my entry. It was a story that I drew and handwrote with a black Bic ballpoint pen. I didn't win the contest or any of the honorable mention awards. Instead, I got a personal note from one of the judges that said, "Jenny, you must really like Pac-Man. Keep writing."

When I was twenty-eight years old, I decided that I would write a self-help book about how to be happy.

But first I needed to figure out how to be happy.

Over the next ten years, I wrote and wrote. I filled box after box with theories and possible content for a book.

When I was thirty-eight years old, I realized that I believed that there was something wrong with me and I learned about the story of the golden Buddha. Together, these two ideas formed the thesis and framework for my book. I decided to write a book that identifies the things that I think are wrong with me and how to see myself as a whole and worthy person. I wanted to learn to see myself as a golden Buddha.

I wrote this book between ages thirty-eight and forty. This is my first book. To learn more about my writing and art, visit www.jennymesserle.com.

Request

Through writing this book, I learned to finally appreciate and love myself for who I am outside of external conditions, such as my behavior and my accomplishments.

I tend to be a private person. But I decided it was more important to publish my book and share my insecurities with others than to keep these examples to myself.

If other people find insight in my words, they may find more ways to give themselves the gifts of self-acceptance and self-love.

* * * * *

If you found my book insightful, please share it with others. Below are a few ideas:

- Ask your favorite health practitioner if you can leave this book in the waiting room for other clients to read.
- Talk with a friend about a story that you connected with and a similar situation that you experienced in your life.
- On a wider scale, share the insights that resonated with you through a yoga class, book club meeting, get together with other parents, Facebook post, blog entry, or email to like-minded friends.
- Ask your library or local bookstore to order the book.
- Write a review on Amazon or Goodreads.

Thank you in advance for your time and efforts.

* * * * *

When we share our stories of shame and inadequacy with other people, we create an environment that invites others to talk about their insecurities. In this sharing, we can view past events as normal parts of life instead of as shameful experiences that should be kept secret. We can see our suppressed stories as just stories and not as indications of who we are as individuals.

When we shed our shame labels, we free ourselves from our fears. We also begin to see ourselves as the whole and worthy people we are and have always been. We are all golden Buddhas!

*   *   *   *   *

"Shame cannot survive being spoken. It cannot survive empathy."[12]
Dr. Brené Brown

Notes

Introduction

1. My description of contentment is inspired by a quotation about happiness from the book *Psychomagic*: Jodorowsky, A. (2004). *Psychomagic: The Transformative Power of Shamanic Psychotherapy*. Rochester, Vermont. Inner Traditions, p. 180.

Section one: The story of the golden Buddha

2. I learned about the story of the golden Buddha from these sources:

   - Solomon, P. (2011). *Finding Joe*, directed by Solomon, P. A Pat and Pat Production.
   - Canfield, J., Hansen, M. (1993). *Chicken Soup for the Soul: 101 Stories to Open the Heart and Rekindle Spirit*. Deerfield Beach, Florida: Health Communications, Inc.
   - Ford, D., Dorman, D., Edwards, C., Evans, D. (2009). *The Shadow Effect: A Journey from Your Darkest Thought to Your Greatest Dream*, directed by Cervine, S. Movies from the Heart, Elevate Films, and Hay House.
   - www.wikipedia.org - Golden Buddha (statue). Retrieved November 2015.

Section two: Childhood messages

3. To learn more about Erin Faith Allen's art, films, and workshops, visit www.erinfaithallen.com. To be precise, the journaling prompt that Erin asked us to complete was "I am too..." not "You are..."

Section two: Special

4. To learn more about Sabrina Ward Harrison's art, books, and workshops, visit www.sabrinawardharrisonart.com.

Section two: Self-fulfilling prophecies

5. In June 2014, I discovered that I believe that something was wrong with me. A few months later, I learned about Dr. Brené Brown's definition for shame. Dr. Brown's explanations of shame made me realize that I have shame and that shame is the term or the name for my belief that there is something wrong with me. My own definition for shame is influenced by the following sources:

- Brown, B. (2012). *Daring Greatly: How the Courage to be Vulnerable Transforms the Way We Live, Love, Parent, and Lead.* New York: Gotham Books, pp.68, 71.
- Shame definition from The American Heritage Dictionary of the English Language. https://www.ahdictionary.com. Retrieved November 2015.

Section three: Gateways to the subconscious

6. See also Rollo May's comparison of anxiety and fever from *Man's Search for Himself*: May, R. (2009). *Man's Search for Himself.* New York: W. W. Norton & Company, p. 27.

Section three: Shame labels and shame sources

7. In Dr. Brené Brown's book, *Daring Greatly*, she discusses "twelve shame categories" which are common areas that people feel shame about themselves. My sources of shame differ from the shame categories that Dr. Brown found in her research. If you are curious about areas of your life where you

may feel shame, Dr. Brown's shame categories may help provide guidance. Brown, B. (2012). *Daring Greatly: How the Courage to be Vulnerable Transforms the Way We Live, Love, Parent, and Lead.* New York: Gotham Books, pp.69, 86.

Section three: The internet and the recycle bin

8. See also Dr. Stephen Covey's definition for responsibility: Covey, S. (1989). *The Seven Habits of Highly Effective People: Powerful Lessons in Personal Change.* New York: Simon & Schuster Inc, p.71.

Section three: Cold medicine

9. The excerpted definition for stupid: The American Heritage Dictionary of the English Language. https://www.ahdictionary.com. Retrieved November 2015.
10. Judgment: Ibid.
11. Comprehension: Ibid.

Request

12. I heard this quotation "Shame cannot survive being spoken. It cannot survive empathy." in this video: *Dr Brené Brown Shame Is Lethal Super Soul Sunday Oprah Winfrey Network*: https://www.youtube.com/watch?v=br9H4LSTJAo. The quotation begins at the 3:34 minute mark. I was granted permission to use this quote in my book.

32902272R00089

Made in the USA
San Bernardino, CA
18 April 2016